AF574196

BACKGROUND MUSIC

ALSO BY CHRISTY BROWN

My Left Foot
Down All the Days
Come Softly to My Wake

BACKGROUND MUSIC

Poems by

Christy Brown

Secker & Warburg · London

First published in England 1973 by
Martin Secker & Warburg Limited
14 Carlisle Street, London W1V 6NN

SBN 436 07093 6

Printed in Great Britain by
Morrison & Gibb Limited
London and Edinburgh

For Mab,

Herself my best poem, and my wife

Towards Morning

For Mab

There is a land above the wind for you to walk through
O my near and inaccessible love.
Green waves for a chariot
clouds to move as shadows about your live uplifted face.

Surf shall frolic among the toothy off-shore rocks
imperturbable background music to our dreaming
happy and lost in this new morning freedom
exquisite on our silent tongues.

Between sky and sea and sand shall be written
in broad brilliant asterisks of truth
the journey that led us unerringly towards morning
caught briefly and forever in a puzzled glance.

The stones will not hurt your feet.
You will come running down the singing shore
and step smiling and sure out of the cold clear morning
into my dream of dreams.

Drinking Song

My flesh sings a jangled rhyme of dying
crying
it sings in the pyre of its bitter burning
turning
to the grotesque gargoyle god of mangled nights and days
always
the terrier smell of my flailed flesh trails after
laughter
beating insanely against the walls of my padded cell
hell
in the last savage twisting of a cork.

Rhyme me a riddle for living.

I open the bright amber river of doom
gloom
exploding into baleful blistered light
height
mellifluously melting and spreading to sky
immensity
a burst bubble boiling and broiling in my bruised gullet
bullet
smashing into the sodden soaken marsh of my mind
blind
under the hounding hooves of oblivion.

Rhyme me a riddle for loving.

Stars dance a mad satanic dance overhead
tread
like demented fireflies in the gutter
splutter
metallic across that hell-bound space
grace

beheld briefly in a woman calmly passing
massing
clouds obscuring the bloodstained city
pity
the paltry wine of this world anointing me.

Riddle me no rhyme at all.

My flesh sings a song of jangled dying
flying
proud above the debris and the loss
cross

of broken bones against the moon.

City Dweller

I have never seen wild Donegal
nor the Atlantic cliffs of Kerry,
though in a haze of alcohol
I might have admired Enniskerry.

I've never dreamt beneath Ben Bulben's head,
or in a pool of poppies hid my face,
and the sweetest poems I have ever read
were down in Christchurch Place.

I've never looked down from the hills of Mourne
to the laughing sea at my feet
for the grandest of scents to my nostrils borne
came from the stalls in Moore Street.

Galway's glories rugged and raw
were in one single afternoon seen,
and the only lakes that I ever saw
were those in St Stephen's Green.

No call of soft-vowelled curlew
came to me across evening leas,
and all the lilting strains I knew
were in The Shaky Man's on the Quays.

Yet my Liffey dreams were just as sweet
as those in a Wicklow valley,
and my heart was first forged in Merrion Street
and blinded with love in Bull Alley.

Distance

Stars both dim and bright
candle-tips or orbs of light
swim in emptiness they say
many a billion mile away.

Many a billion mile and year
before their beam discerns us here
before their beam discerns the part
we would keep hidden in the heart.

In this tangled sphere below
heart cries out to heart I know
and one is dust for many a year
before another heart will hear.

As distant as star is from star
heart is from heart, and twice as far.

Fallen Masonry

Few things are ever mended
by mere touch of expert fingers;
no dream is ever ended
that in the lost heart lingers;
lack of love decreases
the joy of every season
and all the bits and pieces
of self sold for high treason.

We can never quite put away
that which once was ours
or surrender to the clay
the ruins of our towers;
however good the mask
we try on for disguise
we cannot help but ask
the impossible from unanswering eyes.

Each set as far apart
as star is from star
the distance of each heart
is as immeasurable and far
and the wreckage of a lifetime
is endlessly extended;
in her house, as in mine,
few things are ever mended.

Good Friday

In and out among the narrow little ways of the town
    They dragged Him, bearded Man, and the gems of sweat
On His brow glittered like gold-dust
    In the merciless fire of noon-day.
Sticks flashed and thudded dully on straining flesh;
    Taunts, maledictions, words sharp with scorn and hate
Sank as fire into the tired brain;
    Spits bright with foulness ran as lava down His chest,
And the cruel, thin stones of the hillside
    Made the blood run from the stumbling Feet,
Staining the earth with a crimson glory.

    On they dragged Him, the cross's shadow on His back,
Up the awaiting hill, as an animal to the slaughter-house.
    He gazed forlorn, with timeless pity upon the deriding multitude,
Sunk in the agony of betrayal, His denied majesty
    A crown of thorns girding the tranquil brow;
And there, Fatherless, they nailed Him to a beam of mountain wood,
    And the pain-bright eyes gazed into the deeps of all that had been and was yet to be,
Surveying His world, His desecrated Garden, hanging from the cross
    Upon a brooding hill, a bleeding Ecstasy.

Her Absence

Some red-tipped cigarette ends in the ashtray.
That painting she admired of Leeson Street Bridge
now put away in a corner out of view.
The Van Gogh she gave me to study
with an inscription from someone else inside
from her student days that made me instantly jealous.
It seems strange that only the other day
she sat in that creaking old armchair
across the cluttered-up space
smoking rather too much, and chatting,
or slim fingers pensively patting
dark-brown raven's wing of hair in place,
my hunting irreverent eyes zealous
to each line of her in that dark suit,
I for once quite still, quite mute,
the ever-changing heaven of her face
as she read my latest poem in silence
that was pure she-devil hell for me,
light copper-glinting on her bobbed hair
from the window behind her, the chair
that held her pressed-back shoulders
oh, so unconsciously!

The sudden desolate deafening quiet
in the dreaming wake of her leaving,
my heart's April-wild riot
of obscure inarticulate pain,
that uncatchable wisp of perfume
she called by some queer foreign name
lingering faintly, fatally in my room
like many a false alarm of Spring.

There's no one now to say, "take it easy,"
and discuss with mock-serious faces
the high incidence of suicide in marriage.

There's no one now to show my latest poem to
and wait for her to attack or approve
with brown eyes warm with solemn praise.
These are fiercely industrious days.
I am less interrupted now with love.

Finding

I write not in pursuit
but in memory
or in pursuit of a memory.

Something there is in me,
some tenacity
will not let things be,
will not let sleeping dogs lie
and the dead be decently dead.
It is almost an obscenity,
this twisting and turning back
into the twists and turns of the past,
this ardent archaeology of the heart
digging up buried Pompeiis of emotion,
lost mansions of affection.

Sipping iced bourbon
on a mosquito-netted back porch;
burnt caress of sand
under limbs prone in the noon;
wordless drives along white August roads
Harold Johnston motels punctuating the miles
down the pre-dawn day to Boston . . .
so long ago, time or dream
is now open to conjecture.
I am sure of so little –

but this:
the night of the open-air cinema
background music of "The Apartment"
above the crackling intercom system,
the stars a backdrop,
her warm slight body against mine
in the anonymous dark,
then home to coffee and explanations . . .
this at least remains
most blessedly unimagined.

In Retrospect

When you walked down that street
on ordinary feet
no trace of angelic grace
hallowed your pensive face
and your hair, although quite nice,
was not beyond the price
of a beautifying lotion.
And I had no hint or notion
that down that asphalt street
on quite ordinary feet
under a factory-smoke sky above
came the epitome of love.

For what books had never told me, dear,
and what I never knew
was that, when the great day came, dear,
love would be merely . . . you!

In the Theatre Box

All the while they discussed the new play
her eyes explored me;
and when they arose to go
her dress rustled like old leaves
down an avenue of another October.

Invocation

I voyage out
from this embattled colony of thought
to where you rise always upon a moveless tide
always as morning.

This eyeless night of bleak dimensions
cannot kill the brief splendour I knew
the forked fire in my marrow
where you flamed.

From these raw sad inarticulate ghosts
the stunted statuary of my life
you draw me past time and time's dull tyranny
into the harbour of your look.

And I enter quietly sweeping and singing
a small secret song inside my skin
to where your shadowed smile finds me out
in a room full of ordinary mortals.

Reading the unfolding of my fate
in the fine calligraphy of your veins
O long before I knew I was alive
to that high art and most singular pain.

Raging in my bones I called your name:
Joy came.

Last Post

I knew the writing immediately
on the letter,
knew the hand more intimately
than the back of my own;
so many times before had I known
that dry, laconic style
that somehow matched her smile –
it hadn't changed a bit,
and the criss-crossed envelope
with sorrowful Lincoln on it
at a crazy slope
stacked with pages that spoke
of writer's cramp; I broke
the seal and read
the things her heart had said.

It began without preamble –
that too was typical
in lines unlyrical;
recapitulations
of scenes shared – the hectic scramble
of morning classes – afternoons spent
in intellectual argument –
solemn declarations
of mutual hates – grave promises –
loaning of books – rebellious Luther
and ascetic Aquinas – discussing a future
we both believed in – sworn dedications –
no trucking with compromises!

But with time
and time's implications –
for no reason or rhyme –
we had had our innings –
farewells and fresh beginnings –

letters put off – communication
gone stale, unused,
old loyalties abused –
the fierce convictions revoked –
the old free commerce choked –
the insidious infusion
of new blood – unvoiced suspicion
of the past – the gradual intrusion
of personal lives –
husbands, wives –
security, maternity, ambition –
ultimate separation.

We had never bargained for such grim mutations –
yet it was but to be expected –
too taken for granted and neglected –
our trust had destroyed the relation.

Lines for Lioba

On her first visit

I

The small flowers you brought
the morning of your leaving
are a week of age this morning
yet they fill my room still
most sweetly, most eloquently
and bring to my saddened mind
your gentleness strong as flowers
breathing out of your silences.

II

Your hands stirred then;
delicate white petals in your lap
against the soft leaf-brown dress.

III

Your gentleness disarmed me;
pointless my arrows fell
in the clear path of your gaze.

IV

You said little;
we broke from the net of words
the black forest of chosen language
free and familiar upon the bright strand
of our understanding
happy and wise as only we can be
who demand nothing of each other;
we looked with eyes not in our heads
and were not dismayed.

V

The small truth you brought with the flowers
grows strong-rooted in crevices of my heart;
not now forever can you escape into unremembrance;
not now forever can knowledge of you be lost
in a trap of time;
as a flower in my mind you shall grow
and time is kind to flowers.

Lines of Leaving

I am losing you again
all again
as if you were ever mine to lose.
The pain is as deep
beyond formal possession
beyond the fierce frivolity of tears.

Absurdly you came into my world
my time-wrecked world
a quiet laugh below the thunder.
Absurdly you leave it now
as always I foreknew you would.
I lived on an alien joy.

Your gentleness disarmed me
wine in my desert
peace across impassable seas
path of light in my jungle.

Now uncatchable as the wind you go
beyond the wind
and there is nothing in my world
save the straw of salvation in the amber dream.
The absurdity of that vast improbable joy.
The absurdity of you gone.

Looking at a Photograph

God, you looked young!
Yourself and myself outside the United Nations
that glass menagerie of caged animals
that citadel of the world's foolish hopes
that doomed Notre-Dame
with all the world as its hunchback.

I always did admire you in yellow.
It somehow brought out the wild lostness in you
the gay deeply caring forever-young in you
willing to walk forever with a dream.
The fountain behind us was a puny thing
compared to the torrent that quietly raged within us.

The sun was so obvious that day.
It shone through your dress
and rendered me happily blind.
Boats were sighing down the river
cars streaking by in an endless scream
and we alone in our world.

I am indeed alone now
looking across the cluttered spaces of my room
at that captured moment of a happier time
when time was not measured by the heartbeats of a clock
and I did not have to measure my joys
by how much I had left in the bottle.

Lucy

She came clouded in mystery and mysticism
and white Tyrolean stockings
from blue Alaskan wastes
to my city of little infinities
her Joan of Arc countenance flushed
in the fervour of her cosmic faith.

She wrote dreamily for children
of animal simplicities
and golden fireflies dancing above brimming buttercups
and buttermilk afternoons and streams that sang
and a God perched prettily on a tree
in a flowing robe of amethyst.
Not of this world was Lucy-in-Wonderland.

She taught me cosmic acceptance
of all things kind and tragic
marvellously vague and indefinite
her fragile thoughts swimming in cosmic oblivion
desiring nought, possessing all
well versed in Francis Bacon and Annie Besant
her rosy Rosicrucian soul blooming in her eyes.

I heeded her sadly;
there was a nunnery odour about her
that bred despair in me
devoted to her long-dead Bacon
another citadel unstormed
another paradise lost
and I savage and intent
marooned with my lonely passion
barred from that final haven
by a pair of holy-white Tyrolean wool stockings.

What has since become of her
my frail American evangelist
with the lustrous eyes and John-Brown spirit
only God knows
and He isn't perched on any tree.

Meeting

For E. O'K.

Daydreaming it down Henry Street
oblivious of the thronging feet
eyes downcast and remote
dark glimmer of fur about your throat
under a dense, dull December sky
passing me by, passing me by.

Passing me by without look or word
without the merest trace of regard
your Hellenic face hidden behind a cloud
moving like one in an ancient shroud
quiet, deliberate and sad of eye
passing me by, passing me by.

Then you turned and your eyes
found me there in some surprise
and you came back to where I waited
a poor man's Prometheus bound and fated
your eyes alive again, brilliant and fine
you back from your dreaming, I lost in mine.

Lady, step always with sagacious feet
among the temptations of Henry Street.

Poem for Sean Collis

For Han and Bob

You who went so innocently before us
do not forget us in that green-gold world of yours.
You the gay laugh upon the Wicklow wind
smiling boy upon a rainbow
galloping over the morning of your life
blessedly unmet with crippling remembrances
shaming us with your enthusiasms.
Spare us now a thought of quiet love
in all your fourteen-year-old wisdom
you whom death has so dismally failed to possess.

You will always enter through the farmhouse door
laden with clean-cut turf for the fire
bearing warmth of young heart
bearing tokens rare beyond your knowing
for those who knew you too briefly
and loved you too well for jealous time to suffer
yet had unkillable joy in that knowledge.

Gather still turf for that unending fire
from your brighter side of the river
joining us all so improbably as one
over a candle-lit table far from last supper
bridging lives once stellar in distance
through the firefly flaming of your youth
and its dark tongueless ending.

I did not know you well, knowing only your eyes.
And knowing your eyes, knew you.
In some other better time boy on rainbow
beyond the brittle dimensions of now
sup with me again at the same table
and crumble between us the bread of brothers.

Sean of light gentleness and boyish wayward ways
the cloud that darkens your last green hour
hangs over us all.

The Drink

She sat there cosily beside me
twining her slim glass in her fingers
hip against mine in the small booth
in out of the December fog and frost
icy streets and rooftops of cars parked outside.
We sat hip-touching, cosily dreamily drinking
in the merry-making midst of the local citizenry;
bricklayers, carpenters, truck drivers, boilermen
and men of praiseworthy unemployment
downing black-skirted cream-topped pints of stout
like avaricious fishes full to the gills,
in randy currents of man-talk about women,
men with grown-up daughters discussing with phallic famine
the attributes of grown-up daughters of other men,
a geyser-shower of bluer-than-blue jokes
flung prodigally into the smokey air,
true men one and all hunched at the Killiney-rock bar
in varying attitudes of stilted eloquence
becoming less stilted, more slurred with beer;
sloping shoulder, half-moon face,
eyes squinted in comic disbelief, hand slapping corduroy thighs,
bedroom intimacies leaking and lisping
from behind mouth-concealing hand, heads nodding emphatically,
wouldn't tell a word of a lie
and herself big-bellied as usual at home
making the lunch for the morning.
The talking ball tossed back and forth unendingly
like ganseyed kids up a handball alley.

She sat there cosily beside me
twining her glass in her prayer-like hands
hip against mine in the small booth
looking for a moment absurdly and incongruously nun-like
in her dark ankle-length coat and dark scarf.

We sat there till closing time
and only out in the cold and fog and frost
did I realise we hadn't said a word.

Mutability

There is a higher world than this far and strange
where loving hearts are subject to no change
out of our narrow day, the blinkered mind
where no rude remembrance leaves behind
a sour taste on the tongue;
there no shadows move
the hushed eternal expectancy of love
and there above the thunder and the rain
unending love brings no unending pain;
in that place
love alters not with the changing face
but lives forever conquering in grace
imperishable, unspoiled, unsaid –
and dead . . .

And we below who can but understand
the quick electric magic in the hand
weave our little dreams and blithely go
out into the dark of life to know
a brief fugitive pleasure
and bravely kiss –
and think life holds little else than this –
the faint sweet intimacy of fingers
lulling us into spells; nothing lingers
save a scarecrow limping sorrow in the night
and soon that too diminishes and dies
in strong questing hearts and morning eyes
opening unto new and broader light.
It is a truth no willing lips can cover –
mortal love dies with the mortal lover
and we are disenchanted, perplexed and sad –
and glad.

My Brothers

I have eight of them,
some with excellent kind wives
endlessly embroiled in maternity;
others sweethearting a little wearily;
they leave their thoughts undisturbed
and resolve disputes with fists
occasionally broken-skinned
with the laying of Dublin bricks
cemented with less than love;
they talk soccer and mark the form
of fillies both equine and feminine
and fidget behind white collars;
they splutter like candle-wicks
flaring, swearing, roaring to lascivious life,
lovely white violence erupting
in quiet pub corners out of reason
devoid of malice veiled or meaning;
they rant rebel themes intrepid,
observe the faithful observances with middle fervour,
eyes glued to clocks for opening time;
half-drunk, half-dreaming, half in love
they pause, rarely, to peep like mice
through the bamboo of their souls,
creep as marvellous jungle creatures
through the forest of their unacted deeds
in proud profundity of valour;
in words splendid and unprintable
they importune their special demons
to fire their loins with strength
for their not insignificant job of creation: pro.

They walk straight in the sun,
plunder their senses prodigally,
hesitate about being too cautious,
copulate whenever they can;
but most of all they talk.

My Credo As Of Now

I conclude
  all conclusions are superfluous
full stops that never stop in one spot long enough
  to be duly devoured by logic;
truth is forever around the next bend;
  look into the honest face of an imbecile
and therein lies the reflected vacuity of oneself
  mirrored in undiscerning depth and immense;
blissful is the imbecile possessing nothing
  save intimacy of the smallest embryonic pulse
in the tremendous minutiae about him
  which might well be truth beyond assertion
the living of which strides stridently on to madness
  and is therefore worthy of our devout pursuit.

I conclude
  love enters through the eyes
trembles awhile at the fingertips
  and departs as soon as the mouth is opened;
for love's success the taking off and putting on of garments
  is not nearly as efficacious as the putting on
and taking off of masks; the best lovers are clowns.

I conclude
  the hope of every honest man is phallic-cored
and the beauty of one woman is always unequal
  to the beauty of the next;
fortunately for poets.

I conclude
  each existence is a casual tragedy
or an indifferent comedy as the case may be
  sustained only by images of hell
and the last sad lugubrious truth
  that there isn't a damned thing to know except nothing.

My Mother's Son

I suffered long before life taught me
the necessity of hypocrisy –
how you must bend your face to the earth
and your protesting soul to the sobbing earth
though you wander among the stars.
I have some ancient battle scars
to show for those kindergarten days
and some not so ancient.
When I had a God to blame and praise
it wasn't so bad – I was complacent
about the things life did to me
not knowing it was the gaping gaps in my mind
and the black Calcutta holes in my mind
that were to blame for my misery,
my stunted, deaf-mute humanity.
Life is uncompromising.

To know this is to bear it
with a certain slow irony,
a flung-to-the-sky frenzy
with lips tight-pressed against blame,
for there is no culprit to name
but ourselves when nobody's in,
nobody to watch us commit the last sin
and turn away from ourselves, for this
is the ultimate cowardice.

The lapping surf of darkness
eats away into my fearing soul
and when there's no convenient God to enrol
into your category of blame,
you feel at last your own littleness.
Our self-deceit will never be done.
Yet I hope, pluck hope from nowhere
as a child that picks poppies for her hair

and sings to herself when it's quiet.
I am not very brave, and by it
I mean I'm not a silent self-suffering one.
I am my Mother's son.

Nemesis

Somewhere in my mind a demon stalks
at once reassuring and destroying.
With demonic intent it heightens my perception
of a midsummer leaf
a Chinese embroidered teacup
the svelte stripes on an aloof cat
secure in its feline nirvana
rejecting people.
And with the same singular dynamism
my most singular and insatiable demon
narrows my perception to zero
leaves me islanded in oceanic nothingness
blind eyes forever upon some insurmountable peak
till the smallest atom of dust upon the floor
or swaying in the insubstantial spaces of the day
assumes the majestic finality and terror of beginning and end.

Somewhere in my mind a demon prowls
ravaging the last remnants of my sensibilities.
Turning my faltering self to stone
it hoists me high on a makeshift cross
a prey to every season of self-doubt
tossing my mind about with cruel gay abandon
hectic in the haphazard ways of desire.
I speak a thousand tongues faultlessly
with my own farce of a tongue
caught immutably in my own image.
I speak the greatest nonsense known to suffering man
from the dismal dredges of sunken sense
and catch on a rare moment the early morning hope
of something around the corner
behind the oriental blinds
beyond the canalled skein of my closed eyelids
groping towards light.

And I know my demon well
beyond the calling of its name.
A sweet pestilence inside my skin
skying me to Icarus heights
on wings already melting
plummetting me to depths familiar beyond the telling.
My demon is myself and I my demon
joined inescapably in the one shroud of skin.

And come morning I awake to find
the old bastard ruling in my mind.

Poem on a Monday Morning

At least the clock has not expired.
That at least kept faith.
There was a dead fly in that night-long glass of whiskey
and you drank it for the best of all reasons;
there was damn all else to drink.
And now that drowned departed parasite
is now presumably swimming deep in your tangled guts
forever lost in its fly-blown nirvana.
A dreary enough final resting place
even for an inebriated fly.

Pyjamas-less you sit, Gandhi-wise, in the cardinal-red chair
your jaded genitals drooping like dead poppies
on unseen view for the girl who never loved you
gliding back across blanched lawns on razor-keen swings of lisping song
that suburban Beatrice of your mad-cap harbourless middle-years
smiling that sublimely stupid mildly-mad midsummer smile of hers
her strong lean tanned turbulent thighs
casually catapulting you to perdition
over the static of transistorised mayhem
and salmon sandwiches squashed in the sand.

Your thoughts now are demented eels wriggling in a shredded net
slipping and sliding coldly down the thin coil of your memory.
Monday should be a null and void thing struck from Gregory's calendar.
It offends against civilised taste. It has a sour-beer stench.
It is miniature Judgement Day for hardworking honest debauchees
rising naked and Saint-Vitus-struck from our sea-tossed sheets
and assiduously avoiding mirrors.

And that which led us so gaily into full-bosomed temptation
is now a raging volcano rumbling in our ravished bellies.

Grey is the mood and cemetery-grey the colour of the mind
in this sunken undersea world of Monday morning
where even the glad sounds of children at play
grates along the nerves like the scraping of a rusty gate.
And tumbling all crumpled from the womanless bed
the one gleam of promise to hit your inflamed eye
was the over-night tumbler of waiting whiskey
tabernacle of doom and salvation
with that doomed and unmourned fly aswim in its amber depths
butchered in bacchanalian glory.

Yet the clock kept faith and vigil.
It has not ceased speeding up your days.

Rainbow in Exeter

Like all tourists we had to find the cathedral.
Like all tourists we failed.
On the bridge we asked a fine stout open-faced Devonshire bobby the way
and stopping the traffic no doubt impressed with your candidly lost American accent
he gave us directions which we of course blissfully failed to carry out
and ended up once more at yet another petrol station asking directions.

Round and round we went as in a squirrel cage
seeking God knows what road
I dehydrated as ever coveting all the gorgeous pub signs
you stopping again and again to pore over the Esso map
and seek to trace with finely pointed fingernail our ultimate destination
on that sad penultimate day.
With absurd yet amused irritation I watched your face
bent studiously over the map spread upon your knees
and I reminding you that the lights had turned green.
The English sky was smiling most blandly overhead.
Set fair, I thought, set fair.

And then a distant voice in the sky
a distant gentle awakening behind the sudden clouds
a fine graffiti of raindrops on the windscreen
and we both of us looked up a bit startled
at the phenomenon above us.

A gateway! A glorious gateway
opening there above us beyond this traffic-loud moment
a triple-barred rainbow to another land
spreading over acres of sky
welcoming us through
and for us then it was the only true thing in the world.

Laughing, half crying, we passed through that gate in the sky
glorious in the knowledge of ourselves
not having any directions
but sure of our way.

Sunday Sequence

I

A boy and girl walk homeward
their little hour of thigh-white love
quite finished.

II

Half across her in wild Glencullen grass
his nicotine fingers flattering
her buttercup throat
brushing nipples bristling under silk,
thinking it time to say something;
saying nothing.

III

In bed malingering on Sunday morning
rasher-and-egg morning of thronging feet outside
exodus of worshippers from the beehive houses;
sister's nightshroud thrown across bed
redolent of his guilt
recalling white-mice skin of her peeping through
on the whiskey-murdered midnight
blotting out the innocent lust
leaping in wild earth.

IV

Late for Mass per usual! his Mother's voice
trailing him down the street
the Via Dolorosa of the concrete jungle,
the girls articulate in every bone
smiling at the slaughter of conscience;
late for last Mass per usual
but in time for the First Session.

V

"Speak to me, love!"
her cry unspoken because speechless
nibbling at the edges of his mind,
he answering with phallic eloquence only
bruised and breathless in chains of mute passion.
He gazes in dregs of porter, seeking omens
his Ides of March upon him.

VI

Belching home evicted from bar
to cabbage and crubeens greenly afloat
on an inner sea of potent porter;
the afternoon a desert without horizon,
his Mother at fire sewing sock over bottle,
sister curled shell-wise on horsehair sofa
deep in simulated fervour of romance novelette,
dark-silk knees just hidden under skirt
moving furtively, soft rabbits in a wood.

VII

"Speak to me, love!"
that other cry from other mouth unspoken
dropping dully into his mind
a dull plop! of raindrop on mud
signifying nothing but the boredom of being together.
She had looked for flowers
walking down the quiet ways from the mountains,
gentian-red roses everdropping from the walls
of the genteel dwellings,
pricked her thumb on a thorn, cried softly into herself,
he with blind face sleepwalking at her side
stepping blindly down into doom
into the bejewelled bowels of the night city
home to that without a name.

VIII

Christ above his bed gazing down
a sad beggar with hands oozing blood and love;
the red lamp of the Virgin
shedding doom's light on white shoulder of sister
rising above sheet in banal beauty of doom
his spider-soul caught in the web of her growing;
a milkdray rumbles down in the dead street
horse splashing urine, anointing the dawn.

IX

A boy and girl walk homeward
Their little lucid hour of thigh-white love
quite, quite finished.

Sunday Visit

We finally found him
curled up in the chair like a many-wrinkled shell
staring blindly out at nothing
among a gathering of imbecilic fossils
his one good eye fastening fiercely onto life
the hair still sturdy though silver under the old cloth cap.

We finally found him
through all that terrible labyrinth of grey concrete cells
quietly rounding out his days
alone in a morass of moronic camaraderie
his doomed cellmates snoozing and snoring all around
and he with his one good eye defying the shadows.

The tears came then
not soft, but real
the tears of a real man broken by life
groping wildly with gnarled fingers at the straws of life
in that awful room of no life
and the television set blaring forth its banalities
drowning whatever words of comfort our futile tongues could offer.

I had no words for him
no words to span the heartbreak of years
when Samson-like he had stood between us and chaos
bringing to us the small rare trinkets of his love.
I had for him only whiskey
the old bitter gift
the poor tribute of one poorer in spirit
than that jaded near-blind half-deaf soul reclining so tamely
in a wicker chair
in a ward of fearful paralysing resignation
a ward full of already dead people
sleeping as the television blared.

Yet the hand that gripped mine spelled out love
and the raw lovely courage of that old landscaped face
put my feeble pity to shame.

The History Teacher

How shall I ever face her –
How can I disguise
The longing to embrace her,
The unwise knowledge of my eyes?

To burrow in mouldy old books
Devised for the mind's high learning,
When I can't forget her good looks
And the heart in me that's burning!

O strength! Let me be able
To master my amorous seizure,
While Cleopatra sits at my table
And talks on and on about Caesar . . .

The Night Before The Morning After

For Anne

I find myself at the old game
the old absurd ecstatic folly-ridden game
of trying to guess your mind
caught up once more in the eternal question-jungle:
"Will she come?" "Won't she come?" "Maybe not."
One half of me says you will be true to yourself
and lose your way once again.
Another and the more naïve bit of me assures me
you will arrive come hell or stale porter
blaming me as ever for woeful misdirections
and in effect saying with brown-eyed refinery:
"Why the hell pick such an outlandish place to live?"

And no doubt I shall be wordless in your presence
if you can imagine such a phenomenon
and as we self-consciously attempt to pick up long-loosened reins
my eyes upon you will be playing the old remembered ballet
under the heavy drink-laden dream-laden weight of years
almost embarrassing you into temporary disarray.
You won't be fooled, however, knowing me well;
as always you will see beyond the quick foolish clown's mask
far beyond the ready bottle of release, the straw of salvation
the real body alone in his microscopic dust
dreaming dreams forever far beyond his station
studiously looking away from you.

Yet let the old motto endure.
Drink and be merry, for tomorrow we may think.
And that could well spell disaster.

In anticipation of tomorrow
I hope the pleasure we have always found in each other
will outwit the ever-eager hawk of remorse.

Girl, bravely fool me with that old brown-eyed witchcraft
blinding me to the lesser losses of life
and guiding my reason towards the greater humbler gain.

My wish for you upon this wary midnight:
May your life be a warm attendance of light.

The Visit

You came into my night again, Mother,
with quiet undemanding suddenness
hallowing my sleep
hushing the wild drumbeats of my heart
your gentle articulate presence
more real and in life at that deeper-than-death hour
than the bleak barren walls of my mausoleum.

Your face held the broken landscape of my life
fissured with the fierce craters of your love.
Your unfamiliar muteness hung about you as a shroud
in that deeper-than-life hour
knifing me back into life
to meet again the meaner little dying of every day.

I woke down the dark to early morning
to the cold too-new anguish of your absence
bound in the winding sheet of grey normality
and searched in all my blind and bleeding world
for the rare reassurance of your ghost.
And found only my own
absurdly alive
jabbering in a hovel of ruined days.

The Wait

She won't come tonight, old boy.
Tomorrow night, maybe, or some other night
she'll come into my squat untidy room
having driven hazardously through town
and as usual lost her way.
She'll sit across from me in her favourite chair
the one that laments with her every movement;
she'll toss off her spotted scarf
shake out her massed hair
look around as always for the non-existent ashtray
and smoke with her pale pink lips
hand finger-tapping her knee.

She'll read my latest poems,
with bent studious face examine what I have written
in all those desert days since her last visit.
She'll listen as I grow loquacious
listen attentively to my arrogant themes
on life, love and the government;
in our pauses the damn clock will chirrup insanely
like crickets in high grass.

In the backwash of our silences I'll watch her
with slow burnt-out eyes;
the shadows live about her mouth.
her toes nearly visible in the thin red shoes.

Windy Interlude

For Anne:
County Antrim

On that ribbon road in the hills
you wool-jacketed against the heathery wind
above the river and the rock-jumping children
we dissected the bones of old hurts
smiled gravely at ancient beliefs now fallacies
told ourselves brave unhappy things
in sudden audaciousness of heart
I seeing not the uncertain sky
but the ever-changing heaven of your face
my heart glutted on this wonder
you most near, the singing and the gold
and the falling away of things into peace.

The first slow raindrop touched my cheek;
I did not heed at all
peacock-proud by you and incandescent
this moment never to be betrayed
never to be trodden by random treason
a flower on this leaden earth;
your head was bare
leaving your hair to blow in the wind;
upon your sudden remote face O then
a look of immense understanding
as if you knew why the day turned traitor
and the curlew's cry died even as we heard it.

You did not see me then;
something deeper held captive your eye and heart
and made the wild impetuous word die upon my tongue.

Wishful

I want to be free of pavements
and clocks that bully my existence,
newspapers, cars that whisk me like God
descending unexpectedly on me,
buses moving like lugubrious elephants.
I'm tired to death of here, my room,
this spluttering absurd monster-machine
its hammer-strokes recording for posterity
my mind's sudden audaciousness.
I would gather around me soft-sandalled things,
shadows on a burnished lake,
trees bending to the earth in love.
Where, oh where are the beautiful people,
the quick of wit, the clowns who spit
in life's sanctimonious countenance –
the insolent, the indolent, the gay
with sunlight dripping from their hair?
Bus queues, elephantine trucks, merciless clocks
and cheese sandwiches . . .

I'd pawn my immortal soul to wake suddenly
and find a girl's footprints in dew outside my door.

Young Charm

I saw her standing in the rain
eyes dull with hope and pain,
like a scarecrow standing there
a tattered scarf round her hair,
a bottle of meths drained to the dregs,
skirt clinging to mudsplashed legs,
trying to sell her wasted allure;
I hadn't the guts to look at her.

Anne

You came from out the nowhere of the past
with dead leaves in your hands,
and I who had known you alone and near
was dumb in a turmoil of speech.

You came out of a confusion of people
with new flowers in your hands
from out the blue and old gold of October
and I had found you again, but not alone.

At Caragh House

Sitting convivial and confessional
on the sunsplashed afternoon porch
the green cloak of Kildare wrapped around us
drawing our minds together sweet and sure
in a season gone beserk with beauty
under the blaze of Easter
prodigal in its mercies.

Thinking ourselves free
sipping brief peace from the bottle at our feet
passing from hand to flashing hand my ragged bits of poems
under that improbable sky
making a brilliant sunburst of your hair
spilling about your face.

We spoke brave foolish things about ourselves
dissecting life with marvellous dexterity
reckless with that moment's truth
I vainglorious as ever
glorying in your praise.

Only later did I remember the hawk
shadowing the sun
waiting, waiting.

At Closing Time

At closing time
all in the prime
of damp roses and wine
the girl slim-hipped
moist-lipped
wolf-haunted
undaunted
stepped out then
from the beehive of men
pressed her gin-and-lime mouth to mine
hair rare and fine
as blown silk against my face
there in that babel place
outside the pub
the unceasing hub
of the night-lit city
in haste without pity
flowing garishly past.

Her lips, soft, then fast
away into the anonymous night
out of blurred sight
a girl unnamed, unknown,
a stray pebble thrown
into the whirling pool of my mind
leaving behind
no cock's-comb gladness
only a sadness
for what I did not know.

I watched her go,
heard the male talk begin.
the braggart boast of sin.

Yet still the aftertaste of gin
recalls for me
haphazardly
her mouth upon mine
crushed roses and wine
and the low keen of despair
in the wild of her hair.

A Dirge Yet Not A Dirge

Let me look up at the sky
for there's still many a good reason why
I don't particularly want to die.

I keep remembering in rhyme
things that are no more in time
and drowning my sorrows in gin and lime

and thinking of things I'd like to see
under heaven and over the sea
before dull Maturity catches up on me;

A Moore Street "daler" complete with barrow
marching down the straight and narrow
cultured corridors of Harrow;

Pubs with doors that never shut;
literary debates in a watchman's hut
humour shining through grime and soot;

motors fitted with noiseless throttle;
no schoolboy made to read Aristotle;
my best poet friend off the bottle;

girls in wide Summer frocks seen
stretched under the sun in Stephen's Green
healthy and nubile and un-lesbian.

And I would put to the metaphoric sword
the gentlemen of the Censorship Board
until they gave up being Our Lord.

And foreign film-makers who stand
in our green and pleasant land
and show us all to be a pigsty brand.

Oh! for a return to the heroic mood
where every child shall have its food
and every man his favourite nude;

when nobody emits a pious shrill
when somebody gets a vicarious thrill
from their copy of Fanny Hill

and nobody with horror looks
upon those who read proscribed books
and start grappling for them with holy hooks.

And those garrulous young scribes who boast
– let them talk less and work the most
and quit waiting for the Holy Ghost.

A return to the simpler joys
that used to exist between girls and boys
before the advent of the Showband noise;

running barefoot along Dollymount strand
hair in the wind and hand in hand
cooking horse-chestnuts in the sand;

time enough to browse and dream
over a lemonade or ice-cream
fishing for pinkers in a rocky stream;

paddling in water that was shallow
sucking a liquorice or marshmallow
and long, long short-cut through the Hollow.

Ah Time, you unreliable toy!
Even my most innocent pleasure you destroy;
now there's no telling girl from boy.

Yet I must resist the urge
to tether on the tearful verge
and flounder in a soulful dirge

and there's no use grunting like a sow
or a melancholy cow;
the time is always here and now,

so let me be no stone-caster
and though these times may move faster
remember: it's not the station, but the stationmaster.

So let me look up at the sky
for there's still many a good reason why
I don't particularly want to die.

A Lesson Unlearned

Now descends the broad disenchantment
of these thirty-three far-flung years;
the solitary re-enactment
of all I failed to do
but dreamed of most fervently;
things I only half-knew
intensely
in some unvisited corner of my mind
that awoke
when the spell broke
to fantastic star-sprung fears
unabsolved by rite of years;
the brilliant and blind
visions that led on
till deceit itself was done
and my little dog-day won;
the comfortable delusions
willingly believed,
the heartscalding confusions
tortuously conceived
clearing from turgid mist and gleam
to brittle morning beam
showing up the stark
emptiness of my dark.

The ageless battle of ideals
fought across a bar-room table;
useless eloquence unable
to break the thinnest ice;
silk-hissing skirts and stiletto heels
echoes of a paradise
forever coveted and uncaught;
the Arctic wilderness of thought
leading howling on to nowhere;
love encountered here and there

turning from exquisite uncandid eyes
to a sordid compromise;
the endless folly of growing wise
hoarding jealously to ourselves
like volumes unopened on undusted shelves
much knowledge and little faith,
attaining man's high estate
hollowed-out versions of what we
once upon a wild time used to be,
before Reason took its toll
of heart and soul
leaving only the hawk that delves
into any metaphysical hole;
how casually we commit the murder of ourselves!

Yet see how little of wisdom I have learned
for while my several little Romes burned
and love itself was stranded and lost
bitten by a bitter frost,
most illogically I continue to sing
of Love, the only lovely thing.

After-Meeting

When our little rounded moment is done,
When we are far beyond the sun
Of this, our immediate day,
With idle tears and idle fears
We will not grope the airy way,
Plaintive for earth and the kind
Of dreaming we have left behind;
Rather hold hands and run
Down some windy avenue of the sky,
Till some shining corner lie
Awaiting us, and have the fun
Of rolling stars across the floor
To thunder at the Great One's door.
And then, tiring, we will go and find
Some lonely valley between cloud and wind,
Some echoing ghost-beloved nook,
And there, together, read the book
Of that other time-remembered life,
And seek the purpose in the strife,
The pain, and the astonishment,
Why it came and what it meant.
And in the pastures of the sky
We will find ourselves, you and I,
And think each in each, wondrous wise;
Learn that which now the world denies,
And feel, and know, and touch, and see
That which our mortality
So enviously debars
With the opposition of the stars;
And, beyond them, we will find
The sweet conjunction of the mind.
To have, and hold, and know, and say,
And feel, who have laid our hands away,
And see the beauty that never dies,
No longer blinded by our eyes!

So we will weep no idle tears,
Or hurt our hearts with idle fears,
When our little hour is done
And we are far beyond the sun.
There is no need for such, when we
Are ourselves for all eternity.

How to be Bored in Paradise

The sheer monotony of the beauty
just one beautiful day after another
can be rather wearing on one's nerves
even when one is in love.

Looking out at eternal palm trees
and blue blue skies
and hearing the hum of the air-conditioning
can make even the most original couple less original
waiting for the unseen presence
just waiting
is the most boring thing in the world.
Excuse me while I yawn.

Honeymoon

Herself and me not being quite ourselves
under the palm trees and those eternal mosquitoes
which is not at all ourselves
Sunshine every day as prescribed
and us pining for Irish rain
and the weather that draws people from extremes
under an everlasting sky of everyday everydayness
that is known to us alone
therefore we pine for that sky.

For Prince

We met on different sides of the world
boy on a rainbow
yours the better world of innocence
unknown to our meaner fears.

Boy on a rainbow
making our day good and clear
a life unperceived by our atrophied vision
smiling kindly at our ineptitude.

We did not know you with our slight minds
we only glimpsed the rare beauty of the truth
shaming us into the hollow shells of ourselves
much too painfully true to be good.

Dear smiling boy on a rainbow
I see you still standing on the happier side of us
giving us new knowledge of this life
as you held out your hand for a candy.

You will always be with us in the better part of our dreaming
the dark incomprehensible beauty of you
stirring us to efforts beyond our strength
hoping to catch a glimmer of your flame.

You are gone now to a sunnier someplace
and yet you will never be gone
for you are forever in the wind and in the fall of the leaf
and these endure beyond the fragile mind of men.

Boy on a rainbow
in your heaven look kindly on us objects of clay.

On the Beach

For Mab

On the beach today I saw a look of quiet amusement
pass over your skyward-turned face
as if predicting my very next word.

I held out bravely; not a predictable word
escaped my salt-watered lips for at least a minute
as I gravely contemplated the crab in the sandhole.

The sun came out like a warrior
assaulting our fragile skins.
Behind my closed eyelids it veered crazily.

Still I knew you waited so quietly in the sand
for the obvious daily words to gush from me
unstoppable as the weather itself.

The crab wore out its welcome
became assimilated with so much sand.
And still I knew that look was on your face.

No respite from the fierce delight of the sun
no respite from the fiercer joy of you
waiting, waiting quietly by my side.

You won the race for the heart.
Your silence was forever eloquent
so unlike my tortured quest for speech.

Twisting over in the sand
love almost turned to anger because you knew me so well
I almost snarled the lovely words out:

"I love you."

And your eyes mirrored the deeper beauty of it all.

Sitting

Sitting with you in any setting is so lovely
it is still so new to me like each new morning
watching each new wonder cross your face
and I a new arrival to joy
happily caught in that wonder.

Your every movement arrests my mind
bringing my senses instantly awake
and in your very stillness I am aware
of things waving my life restfully
to a joyous conclusion.